Jannik Horsmann

User Acceptance of e-Commerce in the Tourism Industry

D1798719

Jannik Horsmann

User Acceptance of e-Commerce in the Tourism Industry

An Application of the Technology Acceptance Model

VDM Verlag Dr. Müller

Impressum/Imprint (nur für Deutschland/ only for Germany)

Bibliografische Information der Deutschen Nationalbibliothek: Die Deutsche Nationalbibliothek verzeichnet diese Publikation in der Deutschen Nationalbibliografie; detaillierte bibliografische Daten sind im Internet über http://dnb.d-nb.de abrufbar.

Alle in diesem Buch genannten Marken und Produktnamen unterliegen warenzeichen-, marken- oder patentrechtlichem Schutz bzw. sind Warenzeichen oder eingetragene Warenzeichen der jeweiligen Inhaber. Die Wiedergabe von Marken, Produktnamen, Gebrauchsnamen, Handelsnamen, Warenbezeichnungen u.s.w. in diesem Werk berechtigt auch ohne besondere Kennzeichnung nicht zu der Annahme, dass solche Namen im Sinne der Warenzeichen- und Markenschutzgesetzgebung als frei zu betrachten wären und daher von jedermann benutzt werden dürften.

Coverbild: www.ingimage.com

Verlag: VDM Verlag Dr. Müller GmbH & Co. KG
Dudweiler Landstr. 99, 66123 Saarbrücken, Deutschland
Telefon +49 681 9100-698, Telefax +49 681 9100-988
Email: info@vdm-verlag.de
Zugl.: Bremerhaven, Hochschule Bremerhaven, Diss., 2009

Herstellung in Deutschland:
Schaltungsdienst Lange o.H.G., Berlin
Books on Demand GmbH, Norderstedt
Reha GmbH, Saarbrücken
Amazon Distribution GmbH, Leipzig
ISBN: 978-3-639-31060-3

Imprint (only for USA, GB)

Bibliographic information published by the Deutsche Nationalbibliothek: The Deutsche Nationalbibliothek lists this publication in the Deutsche Nationalbibliografie; detailed bibliographic data are available in the Internet at http://dnb.d-nb.de.

Any brand names and product names mentioned in this book are subject to trademark, brand or patent protection and are trademarks or registered trademarks of their respective holders. The use of brand names, product names, common names, trade names, product descriptions etc. even without a particular marking in this works is in no way to be construed to mean that such names may be regarded as unrestricted in respect of trademark and brand protection legislation and could thus be used by anyone.

Cover image: www.ingimage.com

Publisher: VDM Verlag Dr. Müller GmbH & Co. KG
Dudweiler Landstr. 99, 66123 Saarbrücken, Germany
Phone +49 681 9100-698, Fax +49 681 9100-988
Email: info@vdm-publishing.com

Printed in the U.S.A.
Printed in the U.K. by (see last page)
ISBN: 978-3-639-31060-3

Abstract

E-Commerce, trust, electronic payment systems, encryption – those are the terms of the new vocabulary for tourism managers today and in the future. The introduction of e-Commerce has created huge opportunities for tourism companies. Being able to market products in a borderless marketplace to nearly everyone, who has access to the Internet represents a great potential to generate more income. The income generated in the business-to-consumer (B2C) market in Germany is expected to grow by 215% from 46 billion € in 2006 to 145 billion € in 2010 (BITKOM in Stahl et al., 2008).

However, the Internet, respectively e-Commerce has not yet been fully exploited. Customers still seem to hesitate purchasing products and goods via the Internet. Security issues are one of the most important drivers for the resistance to conduct business via the Internet. Customers appear to distrust the new technology due to reasons of fraud, privacy concerns and doubts about the security of networks and databases. Recent incidents like the loss of private customer data (Deutsche Telekom) have definitively not contributed to a change of those perceptions.

This work aims at identifying the major causes, positive as well as negative, affecting the growth of e-Commerce in general and in the tourism industry. Furthermore, the basic components of e-Commerce, such as electronic payment systems (e-Payment), and issues of trust and security are to be covered and discussed critically.

The author intends to apply the Technology Acceptance Model (TAM) by Davies and Bagozzi in order to explain the behaviour of customers and their intention to use e-Commerce in the tourism industry. The underlying data was gathered in the course of a quantitative questionnaire. The resulting outcomes construct a fundament for the discussion of strategies intending to further enhance the application of e-Commerce in the tourism industry. The last part of this work aims at presenting the basis for further research in this area.

Table of Contents

1. Introduction

The following section will explore the relevant fields of interest in relation to the thesis' topic. Aspects and definitions of the area of e-Commerce, (Online or eTrust) trust, electronic payment systems, as well as the current dynamics favouring or hesitating the growth of E-Commerce in the tourism industry will be covered and examined.

The author commences the literature review by providing the reader with a short introduction of e-Commerce in general and its application to the tourism industry. Later on, aspects and characteristics of (online or eTrust) trust will be covered and discussed critically.

The next section deals with the various electronic payment systems currently in use to settle electronic transactions. The author will focus on those systems applicable to the tourism industry. The final part of the literature review covers the opposing factors for the growth of e-Commerce in the tourism industry.

2.1. Introduction to e-Commerce

'Electronic commerce (e-Commerce) is such a service offering people the opportunity to do their shopping via modern information and communication technologies at home' (Schultz, 2007). It enables everyone to conduct business via the Internet. The only precondition is a computer and a connection to the Internet.

The term e-Commerce is becoming increasingly important in the dictionary of today's tourism managers all around the world. This is reflected in the development of the overall online travel market turnover in Europe reaching a total of EUR 70 billion in the year 2008 (V-I-R, Verband Internet Reisevertrieb, 2009). The introduction of the internet represented both, major opportunities as well as threats, for the tourism industry. The internet erased physical borders and enables everyone to participate in a global marketplace. The only requisite is a computer and an internet access. This section explores the current dynamics within the broader area of e-Commerce and provides definitions for the incorporating aspects of business transactions via the Internet.

The worldwide proliferation of the internet led to the birth of electronic transfer of transactional information. 'E-Commerce flourished because of the openness, speed, anonymity, digitization, and global accessibility characteristics of the internet, which facilitated real-time business' (Yu et al., 2002).

One can of course argue, whether the anonymity of the Internet is still valid today. Maya Gadzheva (2008) for example, suggests that the 'achievement of unobservability and anonymity in the Internet is going to be much more difficult in the future, due to the possibility of unlimited collection of data'.

Through the aide of the internet tourism companies are able to market and sell their products to a far greater mass which represents substantial growth opportunities for them. According to Porter (2001), the 'Internet technology provides better opportunities for companies to establish distinctive, strategic positioning than did previous generations of information technology'. However, those opportunities can also represent burdens for companies participating in transactions via the Internet. Those companies are now more than ever forced to keep their web sites up-to-date and to provide reliable information. Since the Internet is a very fast changing medium, it requires their participants, in this case the e-merchants, to keep up with this pace. In case the companies cannot fulfil these requirements, they will probably face a shift of customers to the competition. Especially the area of tourism, being labelled as largely information driven (Morgan et al., 2001) requires constantly updated and reliable information. Customers need to find every information they require on the web. They need to know where to search and they need to be convinced of the trustworthiness and reliability of this information.

The ability to inform clients and to sell and market products in the virtual marketplace is a critical success factor for economic triumph of tourism companies nowadays and in the future. The website is thus a digital business card of tourism companies and one of their most effective sales persons at the same time.

'Internet technology provides buyers with easier access to information about products and suppliers, thus bolstering buyer bargaining power' (Porter, 2001). This will also decrease the costs of switching suppliers (or tourism companies). That is the downturn of the Internet. Competitors are only a few mouse clicks away (Porter, 2001) and the whole industry becomes more transparent. Just about every company participating in e-Commerce is obviously forced to list prices of their holiday components. This facilitates the comparability of tourism services.

Customers do now have access to all kinds of information that facilitate as well as influence their holiday choice. Since tourism companies can no longer differentiate themselves from the competition by pricing means, the corporate website, and the online booking process of a holiday becomes progressively more important. This involves the appearance of the website, including usability and content related features, but also everything concerning the actual booking process and transaction handling.

> The tourism company (the seller) and the customer (the buyer) conducting business over the internet have usually never seen each other face-to-face, nor do they exchange currency or hard copies of documents hand-to-hand. When payments are to be made over a telecommunications network such as the internet, accuracy and security become critical (Yu et al., 2002).

In other words this would mean that customers need to transfer extremely private information like credit card details to a complete stranger.

Summarizing this section it can be said that Internet and e-Commerce present various advantages for tourism customers, since companies and offers are more transparent and easier to compare. Furthermore, improvements in IT technology will enhance the search for relevant information and facilitate the navigation in the World Wide Web.

However, there are also threatening factors for tourism companies. Competition will become stronger, since competitors are only a few mouse clicks away, switching costs for customers are much longer and due to their access to nearly unlimited information the customers' bargaining power will increase. Nonetheless, tourism companies who can keep up with the fast pace of the Internet and who are able to convince customers of the reliability, trustworthiness and timeliness of their displayed offers and information will benefit from the Internet.

2.2. Online Trust or eTrust

What is (online) trust? A first step towards the answer of this question can be made by looking at various definitions of the term trust. Trust is defined as 'the trait of believing in the honesty and reliability of others' (Wordnet, Princeton University, 2006). According to this definition, buyers conducting transactions via the Internet will have to rely on a person or institution they may have never seen or even heard of. This would certainly be not sufficient as an assurance for most of us. Another definition defines trust as 'to hope or wish' (Wordnet, Princeton University, 2006). Summarizing this would mean that we need to rely on the goodwill of the other party and hope or wish that it will act as it was promised. Those definitions might be a good starting point in explaining the meaning of trust, but they certainly do not seem to be convenient for most of us.

Böhle et al. (2000) argue that trust is a precondition for flourishing e-Commerce. Shankar et al. (2002) advance a different view, although they classify '(online) trust as being important in both business-to-business and business-to-consumer e-business'. Koufaris and Hampton-Sosa (2004) pursue a similar way of argumentation. They suggest that 'lack of trust in online companies is a primary reason why many users do not shop online'. Another author, Peter Landrock (2002), founder and managing director of Cryptomathic UK Ltd., one of the world's leading providers of security solutions to businesses, points out that 'without such trust, neither businesses nor consumers will conduct transactions or sensitive communications across this medium (the Internet)'. This argument is being supported by a recently conducted study by Ernst & Young and the Information Technology Association of America who concluded 'that trust represents one of the most fundamental issues impacting the growth of e-Commerce' (Talwatte, 2000). Strader and Shaw (Chadwick, 2001) point out that 'consumers are more likely to buy from an online company they trust, when price differences are small'. Thos would in turn imply that whenever price differences are significant, customers are willing to accept a higher level of uncertainty and perceived risk in transactions with companies they do not know or trust.

According to those argumentations one can say that trust is the major precondition for both, businesses as well as consumers to conduct transactions via the Internet. 'Trust is a key challenge to the customer acceptance of e-Commerce: the lack of trust is an important reason for the hesitant growth in e-Commerce and for the reluctance of consumers to engage in online buying transactions' (Schultz, 2007).

A Forrester Survey from 2000 stated that '51% of companies would not do business with parties they do not trust over the web' (Shankar et al., 2002). However, this would also mean that 49% of companies would do business with companies they do not trust. Trust needs to be strongly combined with uncertainty and ambiguity. The more information a buyer has about the seller, the better can he or she estimates whether the seller will act as it was promised. Thus, the better the information about a seller the better can he or she be trusted. Good examples for this assumption are online marketplaces like eBay or Amazon.

Those two providers offer nearly everyone the possibility to participate in e-Business. Since they recognized the increased need from customers for information about sellers, they introduced up-to-date ratings. Every seller can be rated after transactions whether buyers have been satisfied with the transaction process or not. The higher and better the rating, the more trustworthy is the seller (in a simplified way). These ratings are good indications for (unexperienced) buyers, since they equip them with information about the seller's past performance in transactions. Other ways in creating trustworthiness are so-called trust seals. 'Those seals are issued by third parties to verify the commitment of an e-vendor' (Cook and Luo, 2003;

Hu et al., 2003; Kaplan and Nieschwitz, 2003; Koufaris and Hampton-Sosa, 2004; Loebbecke, 2003; Patton and Jøsang, 2004; Urban et al., 2000; Yang et al., 2006; in Schultz, 2007).

> Trust seals are generally indicated via symbols on the web site of the seller. Those seals are a sign that the seller conducts business according to the standards of the third party, the trust seal provider, and/or that the seller conducts business as promised by the statements and policies on the web site (Schultz, 2007).

'Further measures to increase trust are security features, the availability of alternative payment methods, privacy, security and return policies and feedback mechanisms and consumer communities' (Schultz, 2007). 'Security is the main concern of consumers before engaging in e-business with a seller' (Schultz, 2007; Hinde 1998). 'Sellers need to incorporate certain security features into the design of their web sites in order to ensure the safety of the whole transaction process' (see Credit Card) (Schultz, 2007). Offering alternative methods of payment is another approach of the seller to signal the willingness to adapt to the customers' needs. Being able to choose a method of payment equips the customer with the perceived power over a part of the transaction process.

It is essential to display the 'rules of the game'. Privacy, security and return policies need to present on every seller's web site in order to inform the customer properly. This will not only increase trust but will also facilitate processes in case of complaints or other problems. The provision of customer feedback mechanism (ratings, reply forms, forums, etc.) is another way for customers to increase knowledge and gather information about a seller. The advantage is that customers can exchange with previous customers of the seller. This way they can obtain an objective evaluation of the seller. However, sellers can also manipulate those forums by uploading faked ratings or deleting negative ratings or feedbacks. Again, the customer needs to develop trust in these kinds of information.

Furthermore, customers do also need to develop trust in the IT infrastructure they are using, since this will be the mean of communicating the transactional data between the seller and the buyer. In other words, consumers not trusting the technology they are using for an intended transaction via the Internet will not participate in any e-Business transaction unless they feel confident with the security.

When considering security issues, a public key infrastructure (PKI) that can provide secure authentication on the Internet is an important step towards secure Internet transactions. It can help to build trust, reduce the potential for fraud, ensure privacy and provide merchants with non-repudiation (Böhle et al., 2000).

It is essential for the merchant that the customer can trust him, his connection and Website and the payment system used. Otherwise there will not be any transactions between the two parties.

Summarizing this section it can be said that information is the key to (nearly) everything. A higher level of information about the other transactional party will increase the level of trust, since uncertainty and ambiguity can be erased at least to a certain extent. Furthermore, it is essential to create awareness for technologies and tools needed for security improvements and the development of trust. These tools and technologies can involve 'soft' components like trust seals and customer feedback forums. The 'harder' components are embedded in the aspect of IT infrastructure. This includes improvements in the encryption and network and database security.

2.3. Electronic Payment Systems

Monetary transactions via the Internet do always involve risks and uncertainty. In most of the cases, there is no personal interaction involved.

That means that the customer has to put a considerable amount of trust in the seller's promise to fulfil everything that has been agreed upon during the confirmation of the purchase (e.g. the delivery of the ordered products or services on time, in the right quality and that the agreed amount of money is charged) (Schultz, 2007; Chadwick, 2001).

According to Lammer (2006) 'Electronic Payment Systems or e-Payment Systems may be defined as all payments that are initiated, processed and received electronically'.

The main concern with electronic payment systems is the level of security in each step of the transaction, because money and merchandise are transferred while there is no direct contact between the two sides involved in the transaction. If there is even the slightest possibility that the payment system may not be secure, trust and confidence in this system will begin to erode, destroying the infrastructure needed for electronic commerce (Yu et al., 2002).

The customer is concerned right from the point he is connected to the website of the seller. The risk of losing private information like contact details, credit card or bank account information is a primary concern of the customer. Therefore, it is necessary that both, the seller as well as the customer take care for the security of their own network as well as with the data exchanged during the transaction.

In Germany, there are currently up to ten different electronic payment methods used with varying frequency and success. The author will only refer to those payment systems which are applicable for intangible goods, such as holidays.

The definitions below are based on the work of Stroborn et al. (2004), who were arguing that one way to 'classify different payment instruments is by the point of time when the liquidity effect sets in from the payer's point of view that means the exact point in time when the customer's account is charged with the payment'. 'Following this premise, one can distinguish between "prepaid", "pay-now" and "pay-later" systems' (Stroborn et.al, 2004). Other authors (Yu et al., 2002, Dannenberg & Ulrich, 2004) categorized payment systems with regard to the following variables. 'The first variable is the 'size or the amount of the payment' (e.g. micro-payments). The second variable depends on the 'type of transaction', e.g. credit card, paying via e-mail (PayPal)', etc. It can be argued which of these two different approaches in classifying e-payment systems is the most appropriate. However, the author decides to use the classification of Stroborn et al. (2004) for the reason that this type of classification can be best applied to the underlying topic of this work, due to the following facts.

The ability to differentiate e-Payment systems by the time, the liquidity effect sets in is important within the industry of tourism. Holiday components, especially cruises are oftentimes financed using prepayments of customers. Therefore, it is particularly important for cruise lines to know which of the offered payment systems allow them to use prepayments as financing means. On the other hand, customers do always want a certain level of security, especially when they purchase a holiday, which is certainly not an everyday expense with regard to the amount charged. Therefore, equipping customers with the perceived power of determining the point of time when the actual payment will be processed will result in a beneficial feeling on the side of the customer. This equipment of perceived power is another way of demonstrating willingness to adapt to customer needs. Customers seem to have all under control, since they receive the product before they have to pay for it. So the seller has already delivered the agreed upon product or service.

2.3.1 Pre-Paid-payment systems

The different Pre-Paid-payment systems currently in use in Germany will not be further explained. Systems like GeldKarte, MicroMoney or WEB.Cent are being used to settle small- or micro-payments up to usually € 100. In this respect an application within the tourism industry is of no relevance. According to the DRV (Deutscher Reiseverband, 2008), the majority of holidays booked via the Internet was between € 500 - € 1.500 (55, 1% of all holidays).

2.3.2 Pay-Now-payment systems

'So called pay-now systems debit the account of the customer at the exact time the customer purchases something. Cash-on-Delivery (COD) and debit entry are well established examples today' (Stroborn et al., 2004).

Online Transfer:

According to Monika E. Hartmann (Lammer, 2006) online transfer can be defined as follows:

> These services are embedded in the online shopping process, e.g. via an automatic popup window connecting to the service provider and already containing all necessary transaction details. The customer is invited to choose a payment option and provide his account details. The completed transaction data set will be routed to the relevant payment service provider for authorization. After successful payment authorization the bank (or the

payment service provider) confirms the payment to the merchant so that the purchase transaction can be completed (Lammer, 2006).

COD (Cash-on-Delivery)

COD is usually used for the settlement of amounts for physical goods. Customers order their desired articles over the website of an online merchant. The goods are then delivered by a mail service. In addition to the price of the delivered goods, the customer pays also COD charges to the delivery service. The mail delivery service then mails a money order to the internet merchant. Due to the simultaneous exchange of physical goods and money, COD is said to protect consumer and merchant at the same time. Nevertheless, it is considered not to be cost-effective and awkward for the consumer, who needs to be present for the delivery. Additionally, this payment method cannot be used for goods delivered electronically (Stroborn et al., 2004).

M-Payments (Mobile Payments)

M-Payment is such a service, where the mobile phone of the customer in combination with a PIN number deals as authentication device. Whenever the customer wants to purchase goods or transfer money, he or she is called by a third party, e.g. Paybox (www.paybox.net), on his or her mobile phone. He needs to confirm the transaction with a PIN. The sum of the transaction is then debited from the customer's bank account (Stroborn et al., 2004).

According to a recent study conducted by the Verband Internet Reisevertrieb, v-i-r (2007), only two percent of all holiday purchases have been settled using m-payments. However, this payment method is expected to grow tremendously in the future. This is already indicated by the awareness level of m-payments. Although only two percent had used m-payments to settle their online purchases, more than 23% of all respondents are aware of the possibility of using mobile payments.

Debit Entry

'The process of a debit entry requires the receiver of the payment, the seller, to inform his banking institution to charge the account of the buyer with a certain amount. This amount is in turn booked on the account of the seller' (www.wikipedia.org).

PayPal

With over 150 million registered accounts worldwide (PayPal, 2009), PayPal is one of the most successful internet-based payment schemes.

Authentication is done via the personal e-mail address of the customer in addition to the entry of a password. The amount is then debited from the customer's PayPal account. Customers using PayPal will benefit since they will no longer have to reveal their debit or credit card number. Furthermore, the whole transaction process is speeded up due to the fact that customers no longer need to enter their address details. PayPal also promotes its product as being more secure in comparison with other e-payment schemes.

2.3.3 Pay-Later-payment systems

'In terms of pay-later-systems (e.g. credit cards), the customer actually receives the goods before being debited' (Stroborn et al., 2004). However, this depends upon the point in time when the customers' bank account is being debited. It is also possible, particularly within the area of tourism that the bank account is debited before the holiday is 'consumed'. Within the tourism industry it is a common practice to book and purchase holidays long time in advance. Especially in terms of family holidays, customers like to book in advance, since they do only have a small time frame (namely the school holidays) where they can go on holiday. So, holidays in these periods are strongly demanded. Thus there is an incentive for customers to book as early in advance as possible. In this case, the classification of Stroborn et al. (2004) is not valid anymore. The holiday is purchased long before it is consumed and thus the bank account will also be debited before the consumption.

Credit Card

'Settling payments via the use of the credit card is the most commonly used payment method worldwide. Nearly 90 % of all items and goods purchased via the Internet are paid by credit card' (Dannenberg & Ulrich, 2004). Stroborn et al. differentiate between three basic ways of credit card payments via the Internet:

1. An unsecured transaction

2. 'A transaction via Secure Socket Layer (SSL), which is a sort of digital envelope. SSL is the de facto standard for secure online transactions, preventing eavesdroppers from learning customers' account details' (Ashrafi & Ng, 2009). The SSL technology establishes a secure communication channel between the participants of an online transaction.

3. 'a transaction employing Secure Electronic Transaction Protocol (SET), which is currently considered as the safest credit-card-based payment systems on the Internet' (Stroborn et al., 2004).

Recapitulating this section again highlights the importance of awareness. According to Monika Hartmann (Lammer, 2006) 'many payment solutions did not succeed in reaching a critical mass of users'. This can be seen in within the example of M-payments. Payment methods may be very useful, however if they do not manage to reach a critical mass of users, they will not succeed in the market. So customers need to be enlightened about the different payment methods available and the advantages and disadvantages involved. In addition the aspect of trust reappears in this section. Customers need to trust the security of their Internet connection in the first place before they are conducting any business transactions.

3.1 Factors favouring the growth of e-Commerce in tourism

The introduction of the internet as well as the ability to pay for goods and services via electronic payment systems created potential advantages for customers as well as for tourism companies. 'The marketing of an intangible product such as tourism largely depends upon visual presentation' (Morgan et al., 2001). With the Internet, marketers finally found the perfect tool. The capability of combining the presentation of facts and figures, emotional pictures and the whole booking process is a huge asset for tourism companies. Buhalis (Morgan et al., 2001) stated that 'organizations and destinations which need to compete will be forced to compute'. Thereby, he assigns companies participating in e-Commerce a significant competitive advantage.

According to a recent study of the VIR (Verband Internet Reisevertrieb, 2007) customers value the easy and fast way of booking trips via the internet. Furthermore, they appreciate the possibility to customize their trips, to see if their desired holiday is still available and the extensive range of offerings. The possibility to pay per credit card and the savings in terms of time they need to invest are also big advantages for German customers booking their trips and holidays via the Internet.

Cheyne et al. (2006) suggested that 'the Internet is providing the means for suppliers and consumers to bypass the travel agent and interact directly'. Furthermore, many writers propose that 'the Internet furnishes travel consumers with more information, quicker responses and often lower prices than they can achieve when making travel arrangements through a traditional travel agent' (Cheyne et al., 2006).

Tania Lang, a senior consultant at Cap Gemini Ernst & Young, stated in her work in 2000 that 'there are a variety of factors providing advantages and benefits for the users of the Internet'. Amongst those factors is the access for availability enquiries and bookings when consumers want to research and purchase travel. Customers are no longer restricted to the opening times of their local travel agency.

According to Buhalis (Lang, 2000), 'the ability to access information which is detailed and up to date assists the travel consumer by making the product more tangible in their mind'. Another important advantage of e-Commerce in tourism is the bypass of travel agent fees and the access to online discounts. Lang (2000) stated that there is a 'cost advantage in purchasing travel online as a result of the market becoming more competitive. These cost advantages can also be explained by decreasing distribution costs'.

Concluding this section it can be suggested that customers will benefit tremendously from e-Commerce in the tourism industry. They will be faced with lower prices, since no intermediaries are involved any more so that potential cost savings can be achieved. In addition to this, the authors cited above implied that the visual representation of holidays will improve due the recent and upcoming developments in technology. According to this, there should not be any disadvantages for customers and conducting bookings via the Internet are the best solution for the future.

However customers will also have to sacrifice in certain aspects as well as they will have to experience that bookings holidays via the Internet might not be that advantageous as the following section will point out.

3.2 Factors for the hesitant growth of e-Commerce in tourism

In 2009, Prashant Palvia argues that 'the Internet is far from achieving its potential due to the reluctance of consumers to engage in its use'. Palvia (2009) stresses this assumption by a recent study, indicating that sales of online retailers were only 2, 2% of total goods sold in the U.S. in 2005. Moreover, analysts have predicted that even by 2011, e-Commerce sales would only account for only 7%. According to Tania Lang (2000), there are certain barriers or disadvantages of the Internet and the World Wide Web (WWW) for consumers. Amongst those factors, the 'lacks of a human interface and of confidence in the technology as well as security issues have a high relevance'. There are a lot of situations, where a customer has built a strong relationship to his travel agent. For some travellers, the actual booking process (whether via a travel agency or the Internet) is already part of the holiday itself. The booking process might even be some kind of ritual which is carried out in exactly the same manner every time the customer goes on holiday. Those loyalty or relational factors are hard to be erased or replaced by the Internet which is in fact a major threat to electronic commerce in the tourism industry.

A number of authors maintain that 'travel agents provide better services, especially when more complex products are to be purchased' (Cheyne et al., 2006). 'Those complex travel arrangements are more information intensive and therefore needs consultation of travel agents compared to less complex holiday components such as flights or rail tickets'. Other authors, including Inkpen, Lyle and Paulson (Cheyne et al., 2006) argue that 'travel agents can offer a more personalized service and provide unbiased advices that add value for the customer'. Concerning the latter assumption one can argue that this is true for inexperienced or first-time users. Customers, who are familiar with the Internet and know where to find the information they are looking for, will not need the advice of the travel agent no more. First of all, the travel agent might provide them with information they already know or find by themselves. Secondly, travel agents are biased too, regarding the amount of commissions they receive for the sale of products. Another case where customers do not need the advice of the travel agent are repeated holidays, meaning customers who always travel to the same hotel. Those customers will not benefit from a travel agent's consultancy. Summarizing this, one can say that 'the service offered by travel agents is value adding for customers, who are inexperienced with the process of online booking and for customers who want to travel to a variety of different destinations' (comparing Cheyne et al., 2006).

The lack of confidence in the technology as well as the mistrust in security are the two other major disadvantages of the Internet that Tania Lang has determined. She points out that the 'main barrier stopping consumers from booking travel via the Internet is the perceived lack of a secure payment method' (Lang, 2000). 'The main concern with electronic payment is the level of security in each step of the transaction, because money and merchandise are transferred while there is no direct contact between the two sides involved in the transaction' (Yu et al., 2002).

'If there is even the slightest possibility that the payment system may not be secure, trust and confidence in this system will begin to erode, destroying the infrastructure needed for electronic commerce' (Yu et al., 2002). Putting this in other words, tourism companies may have the perfect product in terms of price quality ratio. However, the company will not be able to sell its products to a greater mass if their payment system is lacking security. This will not only erode trust in the payment system itself, but may also affect the customers' acceptance of the company, thus affecting the company's reputation, image and profits.

In 1998, Haas surveyed that even though 'many Internet users go online to find product information, most users prefer to log off and buy their goods through traditional sales channels'. Of course, this trend has increasingly changed over the last years; however, still today customers inform themselves over the Internet without performing the actual purchasing process online. The main message which is included in the statements of both of them is the fact that an 'increase in the safety and security of electronic commerce will have a tremendous impact on the online purchase behaviour of tourism customers' (Haas, 1998).

Another important point is that 'while customers may be happy to purchase small consumer items via the Internet, such as books and CDs, they may not be ready to make larger, pricier and more intimidating purchases online such as travel and tourism services / products' (Lang, 2000). Lang's findings are confirmed by a comparable study in Germany performed by the Ifak Institut (Institut für Markt- und Sozialforschung).

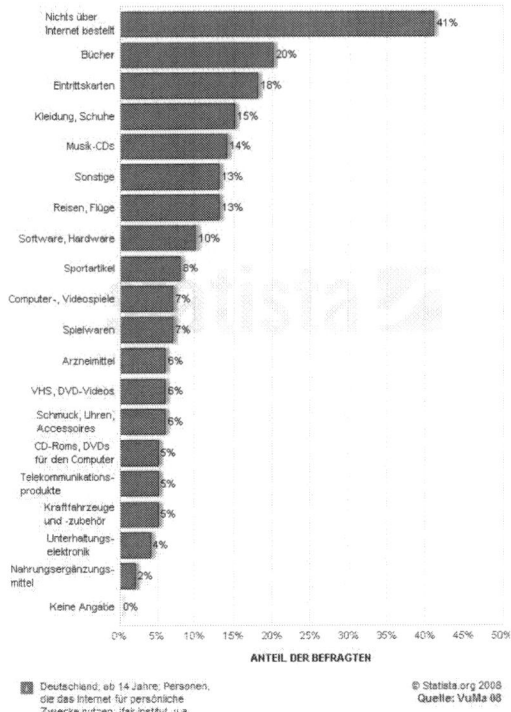

■ Welche Produkte oder Dienstleistungen haben Sie
bereits über das Internet bestellt bzw. genutzt?

Nichts über Internet bestellt	41%
Bücher	20%
Eintrittskarten	18%
Kleidung, Schuhe	15%
Musik-CDs	14%
Sonstige	13%
Reisen, Flüge	13%
Software, Hardware	10%
Sportartikel	8%
Computer-, Videospiele	7%
Spielwaren	7%
Arzneimittel	6%
VHS, DVD-Videos	6%
Schmuck, Uhren, Accessoires	6%
CD-Roms, DVDs für den Computer	5%
Telekommunikations-produkte	5%
Kraftfahrzeuge und -zubehör	5%
Unterhaltungs-elektronik	4%
Nahrungsergänzungs-mittel	2%
Keine Angabe	0%

0% 5% 10% 15% 20% 25% 30% 35% 40% 45% 50%

ANTEIL DER BEFRAGTEN

Deutschland; ab 14 Jahre; Personen,
die das Internet für persönliche
Zwecke nutzen; ifak institut, u.a.

© Statista.org 2008
Quelle: VuMa 08

Fig 1. Frequency of products / services purchased via the Internet in Germany (Statista.org, 2008)

In this survey, holidays and trips booked over the internet are still ranked lower than books, clothes and CDs.

Summarising this section it becomes clear that trust does again play a crucial role in the formation of successful online transactions. Furthermore, the factor of personal consultation is important to many customers, especially when it comes to complex products. Last but not least, the payment methods offered by a tourism company can affect the customers' decision of conducting business via the Internet.

4. Research

The aim of this research is determine the major factors that hinder the growth of e-Commerce in the tourism industry. Furthermore, solutions to these problems should be identified, in order to give recommendations to the industry. Through the aide of statistical analysis, the researcher aims to detect potential characteristics or patterns of e-Commerce hesitators. The underlying assumption is that especially older people tend to resist using e-Commerce in the tourism industry due to a high level of computer illiteracy. This would be a beneficial finding for the industry, since they would know on which demographic groups they need to focus on as well as to which items or steps in the booking process they need to focus their attention on.

The method used for this kind of research will be of quantitative nature. A structured questionnaire will be used which consists of closed-ended questions for the most part. These closed-ended questions will mainly be ranking questions, where the respondent has to choose the answer which is most appropriate for him from a range of, usually five, possibilities or options. Therefore, a five-point-Likert scale was applied to the greater part of the questions.

The questionnaire will be composed of demographic questions and questions concerning the computer literacy of the respondents and their attitude towards e-Commerce applications within the tourism industry. Additionally, there will be opportunities for respondents to include more qualitative information through the provision of a comments field. Part of the questionnaire will also be a short introductory message that outlines the aims of the research, as well as an assurance that all responses will be kept strictly confidential.

Before the actual survey is carried out, a pre-testing of the questionnaire will be conducted. The outcome or major goal of this pre-testing phase is to clarify whether the questionnaire is clear in terms of wording, layout and comprehensiveness. The testing group will consist of friends, relatives and study colleagues. The size of this group will not exceed ten persons.

The method of pre-testing the questionnaire will guarantee that it will be understood by all respondents. Furthermore, changes can be made beforehand, thus they will not affect the results of the questionnaire.

The actual research will be carried out via an online questionnaire. The link of this questionnaire will be sent out to selected contacts of the researcher (approximately 30). The underlying assumption is that the respondents addressed will forward the questionnaire to their contacts. The result will be some kind of snowballing effect. This would promise a random sample including respondents who belong to a variety of demographic groups.

The researcher aims to achieve a sample size of at least 50 or more respondents. The study population will consist of adult (over 18) internet users, since the questionnaire can only be worked on via the Internet. The questionnaire was started on the first of June 2009 and lasted for 21 days. Within this period, 109 completed questionnaires were collected.

4.1 Research Methodology

The conceptual framework used for this study is the Technology Acceptance Model (TAM) developed by Fred Davis and Richard Bagozzi in 1989. 'It is one of the most influential extant research models designed to explain user's technology acceptance behaviour' (Kim et al., 2009). 'The TAM is based on the social cognitive theory of reasoned action (TRA) by Fishbein and Ajzen (1980; 1975)' (Park et al., 2009) and 'the theory of planned behaviour (Ajzen, 1985)' (Ha and Stoel, 2009). 'It aims to predict and explain user acceptance of information systems (IS) or information technology (IT)' (Shih, 2004). The TAM is based on two major variables, namely the perceived usefulness and the perceived ease of use of a new technology. Both factors strongly influence a person's attitude towards a new technology, thus determine the persons' intention to use the system or technology. Additionally, the 'TAM also incorporates a causal relationship between the two variables, suggesting that an individual's perception of how easy or difficult it is to use a system will influence his/her perceptions about the usefulness of the system' (Vijayasarathy, 2004).

'By knowing which web site attributes influence consumers' beliefs about online shopping, e-retailers can improve their e-shopping sites and thus enhance more customers to book or buy via their web sites' (Ha & Stoel, 2009).

The first variable, perceived usefulness (PU) is described as 'the degree to which one believes that using a particular system or technology will enhance his or her performance' (Davies, 1989 in Shih, 2004). Whereas the other variable, perceived ease of use (PEOU), refers to 'the degree to which one believes that using a particular system would be free from effort' (Davies, 1989, in Shih, 2004). After 'revising Davies' definition of PU, the PU of e-shopping is defined as the degree to which an individual beliefs that trading on the Web would enhance the effectiveness of his or her shopping' (Shih, 2004). Shih (2004) also differentiates 'PEOU into two different parts: PEOU of the Web and PEOU of trading on-line'. Since the process of purchasing holidays on-line does include both components, namely the information search (PEOU of browsing the web) as well as the aspect of trading or purchasing (PEOU of trading on-line) the author decided to stick to the original PEOU definition of Davies. So there will only be one overall variable, namely PEOU which incorporates the aspects of both, trading and browsing on the Internet.

Although the TAM has been applied in various previous studies in related areas of interest before (Ha and Stoel, 2009; Lee, 2009; Shih, 2004; Kim et al., 2009) the author expects it to be the best model in explaining customers' reluctance to the application of e-Commerce in the tourism industry. Furthermore, there has not been an application of the model to the appliance of e-Commerce within the tourism industry so far.

As previous studies (Vijayasarathy, 2004; Li & Lai, 2005; Shih, 2004) have revealed, 'perceived ease of use has a positive effect on the perceived usefulness'. That means, that whenever the user has the feeling that the use of a particular system can be done without any hassle, it will have a positive effect on the perceived usefulness of that particular system. In other words, the easier and uncomplicated the usage of a system, the higher will its perceived usefulness be.

Like other researchers (e.g. Kim et al., 2009) the author will extend the existing TAM by a third variable, namely perceived trust (PT). Similar to the fact that perceived ease of use will positively affect the perceived usefulness, the author assumes that perceived trust will also be positively correlated with perceived usefulness. As mentioned before, trust is a major challenge to (tourism) companies conducting business over the Internet. According to Shankar et al. (2002), 'the lack of trust is one of the greatest barriers inhibiting online trade between buyers and sellers who are unfamiliar with one another'.

4.2. Testing Hypotheses

Hypotheses 1:

Perceived Usefulness (PU) positively affects a User's intention to use a new technology.

Hypotheses 2:

Perceived Ease of Use (PEOU) positively affects a user's intention to use a new technology

Hypotheses 3: Perceived Trust (PT) positively affects a user's intention to use a new technology

4.2.1 Perceived Ease of Use

Hypotheses 4:

Speed positively affects Perceived Ease of Use (PEOU). The variable speed can be best illustrated by the number of mouse clicks a user needs in order to make a booking. It also implicates 'the speed, with which users can find what they are looking for' (Flavían et al., 2006). It is advisable for companies to assign a high priority to the aspect of speed. Online sellers have to minimize the number of mouse clicks needed to perform a booking. Every additional click might cause annoyance on the side of the customer and adds a new level of complication. An increase in the number of steps involved in an online booking does also cause a higher risk of losing potential customers during the process. The more a seller reduces the number of mouse clicks necessary to successfully complete a booking via his web site, the more satisfied will the user be with the whole booking process.

Hypotheses 5:

Simplicity positively affects Perceived Ease of Use (PEOU). Simplicity can be defined as the ease with which a user can navigate through the website. An increase in simplicity will automatically lead to an increase in user satisfaction. According to Palmer (Zviran et al., 2006) 'user satisfaction […] has been found to be significantly associated with usability features unique to the Web, such as download delay, navigation, content, interactivity, and responsiveness'.

Hypotheses 6 a:

Easy and secure payment methods positively affect Perceived Ease of Use (PEOU). 'Many innovative payment methods never succeeded in the market, since they have not generated a critical mass of users' (Hartmann, in Lammer, 2006). With regard to a recent study performed by the IWW (Institut für Wirtschaftspublizistik, in Dannenberg & Ulrich, 2004) results indicated that 61,3% of respondents choose among different payment methods on the basis of the criteria' easy handling'.

Hypotheses 7:

Experience in computer-usage (Internet) or computer literacy positively affects the Perceived Ease of Use (PEOU). Users who have already made experiences with computers, the Internet and e-Commerce are believed to have a much lower level of frustration. They are able to cope with problems and tackle potential complications within the booking process. Thus, it will appear to them, that using the system is easier compared to users with no or minor experiences in computer usage.

Hypotheses 8:

Experience with online bookings positively affects Perceived Ease of Use (PEOU). Frequented repeating of online booking implies the development of routine and loyalty in using the system and the payment methods offered. Especially in terms of payment methods used, customers develop a strong loyalty to those systems. Having made the experience of a successful transaction will increase the trustworthiness of the system used and will in turn increase the switching costs to other systems.

Hypotheses 9 a:

Access to constantly updated information concerning the availability of products and services positively affects Perceived Ease of Use (PEOU). Having access to real-time data about actual availabilities of holiday components decreases the level of frustration for potential customers. Knowing in beforehand which products are still available will result in time savings, since customers will not have to repeat the whole booking process again.

Hypotheses 10 a:

Ability to conduct bookings without time restrictions positively affects Perceived Ease of Use (PEOU). The ability to book without being timely restricted by opening times (e.g. travel agencies, call centres, etc.) will provide potential customers with the freedom to decide on their own when to perform a booking. This would erase the pressure to take a decision within the time frame of opening times.

Hypotheses 11 a:

An easy search for relevant and required information positively affects Perceived Ease of Use (PEOU). With the introduction of search engines and search functions embedded in websites, the process of finding appropriate and relevant information has been facilitated a lot in the recent years. This factor is believed to have a positive influence on the Perceived Ease of Use (PEOU).

Hypotheses 12 a:

Web site design will have a positive effect on Perceived Ease-Of-Use (PEOU). A well-structured Web site, including aspects of navigation, content, aesthetics, and usability can facilitate the process of finding relevant information and booking a holiday in general. A Web site that is well-designed can even assist inexperienced computer- or Internet-users in finding the relevant information and guiding them to the booking of a holiday. This will also reduce the potential for frustration on the side of the customer.

4.2.2 Perceived Usefulness

Hypotheses 9b:

Access to constantly updated information concerning the availability of products and services positively affects Perceived Usefulness (PU). The ability to know which products are still available decreases the perceived power of the travel agent and in turn equips the customer with more information. Some years ago, travel agencies were the only ones having access to availabilities of holidays. Thus, they had a more powerful position within the customer - travel agent relationship due to their 'expert knowledge'. Nowadays, everyone can access databases or browse through travel portals and instantly see what holidays are still available. The ability to detect vacant products (e.g. hotel beds) will put the customer in a far better position. He or she no longer depends on the travel agent's expertise. This factor is believed to have a positive influence on the Perceived Usefulness (PU).

Hypotheses 10 b:

The ability to make bookings without time restrictions (e.g. opening times) will positively affect Perceived Usefulness (PU). Customers do not have to invest time and money to get to their local travel agent. This will provide them with the feeling of a more efficient booking process. Since the Internet can be regarded as a 24/7 travel agency with no defined opening times, customers can book their holidays whenever it suits them best.

Hypotheses 11 b:

An easy search for relevant and required information positively affects Perceived Usefulness (PU). Customers do no longer have to skip pages in numerous travel brochures in order to find what they are looking for. Through the introduction of the Internet and e-Commerce to the tourism industry the customers do now have only one page they need to look at, namely the screen of their computer. Relevant information can be brought up screen by just a few mouse clicks. Customers do no longer have to switch between pricing sections and holiday descriptions in brochures. Everything can be displayed centrally. This development is believed to have a positive influence on the Perceived Usefulness (PU).

Hypotheses 13:

Access to a variety of information positively affects Perceived Usefulness (PU). Sheldon (Lang, 2000) already identified the tourism industry as being highly information intensive. Given the special characteristics of holidays being an intangible service / product, it heavily relies on detailed and up to date information to evoke emotions and positive feelings on the side of the potential buyer. In 2004, Shih argues that 'consumers expect websites to support their shopping on the web, or in other words, consumers may require accurate and available information on target products and services'. He concludes that the quality of information can have a positive influence on e-shopping behaviour.

Hypotheses 14:

I believe that booking holidays via the Internet saves me time. This statement is positively related to the Perceived Usefulness (PU) of e-Commerce in the tourism industry. Customers, or users, positively responding to this statement perceive that booking holidays via the Internet possesses a tremendous potential to save time. Especially nowadays, where more and more people get stressed while they are trying to fulfil all the appointments of their agendas, potential opportunities to save time become increasingly important (e.g. Fast food, online shopping, home banking, etc.). Introducing e-Commerce to tourism, people are now able to book their holidays in their lunch breaks, or even via their mobile phones. They do no longer have to visit a travel agency and have an extensive and time-consuming conversation with the travel agent. This development is believed to positively affect Perceived Usefulness (PU).

Hypotheses 15:

The timeliness of Information affects my purchasing decision. This statement is positively related to the Perceived Usefulness (PU). Tourism companies cannot afford to display outdated information. This would lead to frustration and denial of the company on the side of the customer. Information on the Web needs to be reliable. Customers do not want to be bothered with wrong information as their holidays should represent a stress-free time. The timeliness of information is positively affecting the Perceived Usefulness (PU).

Hypotheses 16:

Transparency of offers and companies positively affect Perceived Usefulness (PU). The ability to find the cheapest offer via the use of automated search engines increases the bargaining power for customers and again decreases the dependability in the relationship between the customer and the travel agent. In addition to this, customers are able to compare between different companies. Through the introduction of travel portals like opodo.de or expedia.de the process of finding the right product for the best price will be facilitated and a lot more faster. These portals can be regarded as personal assistants or digital travel agents. With their help customers can erase potential disadvantages of online booking. Since they can no longer receive advices from their travel agent they can benefit from the 'expertise and knowledge' of the databases of those travel portals. Customers do not have to rely on their travel agents, promising them the best price for the best quality.

4.2.3 Perceived Trust

Hypotheses 6 b:

Easy and secure payment methods positively affect Perceived Trust (PT). Providing customers the opportunity to choose among different payment methods is expected to result in a beneficial effect concerning the transaction process. Customers can now choose the payment method they feel most comfortable with. This is a major precondition for a successful transaction. Since the transfer of money can be regarded as one of the most critical points in the booking process, it is important that customers are furnished with the perceived power of deciding which payment methods is being applied. This will increase customers' trust in the company on the one side, but will also lead to a more comfortable and satisfying experience for them. By choosing their favourite payment method, customers make sure they are using the one they are most comfortable with and expect it to be the most secure one.

Hypotheses 12 b:

Web site design will have a positive effect on Perceived Trust (PT). Kim and Moon (Chadwick, 2001) found out that 'perceptions of trustworthiness can be manipulated by varying the design of a Web site, particularly the use of graphics and colour. Web site design also includes the aspect of content'.

Hypotheses 17:

Security and encryption of Internet connection will positively affect Perceived Trust (PT). As mentioned before 'customers need to trust the technology they are using as well as the payment system applied and the other parties involved in the transaction process' (Shankar et al., 2002). The higher the level of trust is the more likely will the customer be to purchase or even re-purchase via the Web site of the merchant. In surveying attitudes toward Internet-based e-banking, Liao and Cheung found that 'system security is a significant determinant of customer attitudes toward system use' (Shih, 2004).

Hypotheses 18:

Reputation of the company will have a positive effect on Perceived Trust (PT). In case the seller distributes his products online as well as offline the offline reputation will have a strong impact on the customer's decision to purchase a product via the Web site. Furthermore, the larger a company is the more reliable are its products. A larger company will also have higher monetary assets to invest into IT security infrastructure. Jarvenpaa et al. 'argued that the reputation (i.e., social influences/subjective norms) of the parent companies, in this case, can provide a cue for the evaluation of the reliability value of the sites to the consumers when they visit Internet shopping sites' (Kim et al., 2009)

Hypotheses 19:

The security of private data positively affects Perceived Trust (PT). As pointed out earlier in this work, customers are greater than ever concerned with the security of their private data (including bank account information, contact details, etc.). Furthermore, incidents of online fraud have increased tremendously over the last years. An increase in the security of private data is expected to lead to an increase in e-Commerce.

Hypotheses 20:

I trust the security of my current network. This statement is positively related to Perceived Trust (PT). Customers who do not trust the security of their network will definitely not participate in online transactions. This aspect of trust can be defined as one of the major preconditions for successful e-Commerce.

Hypotheses 21:

The security of my privacy affects my purchasing decision. A positive response to this statement will affect Perceived Trust (PT). Customers are concerned whether their privacy is still secure nowadays. Recent affairs (e.g. Telekom) where databases containing customers' private data have been hacked and data was stolen add fuel to this concern. 'Anonymity of online purchases and visits of Web sites is another worry of many customers today. They simply do not want that their online behaviour can be traced, due to spamming, identity theft, and so on' (Gadzheva, 2008).

Hypotheses 22:

I believe that most online sellers are trustworthy. Positive responses to this statement are a major precondition for online transactions to be materialized. As Koufaris and Hampton-Sosa (2004) suggested, 'lack of trust in online companies is a primary reason why many users do not shop online'. It is believed that this aspects positively affects Perceived Trust (PT).

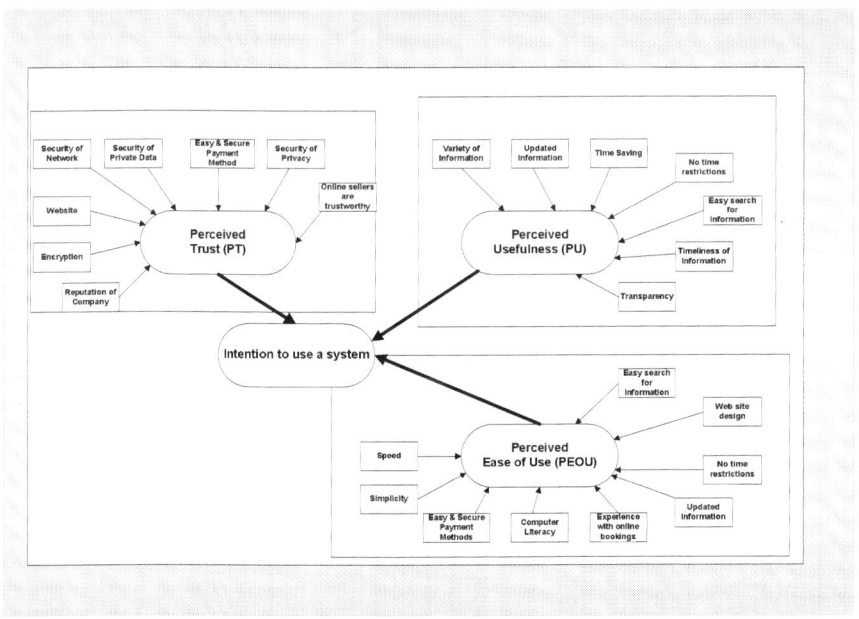

Fig. 2 TAM Adoption

5. Results

5.1. Demographics and Computer (Internet) Literacy

The mean age of all respondents was 33.05 with ages ranging from 19 to 74. The majority of all participants, 90, 8%, had an educational level equal to Abitur or above (Master, Bachelor, Diploma). 54, 1% of all respondents were male. The greater part of all respondents has an income up to 3,500 € per month. On average one can say that all respondents are familiar or very familiar concerning their experience with the Internet (53, 2% very familiar, 42, 2% familiar). This is also be demonstrated in the experience with online bookings, where 90, 8% of all respondents had already booked a trip (rail-, flight-tickets, etc) via the Internet.

The most popular holiday type (multiple answers were allowed) amongst the respondents were city trips (60 mentions), All-Inclusive (32 mentions) and others (41 mentions). The majority of respondents (59, 6%) spend between 600 - 2.000 € per person and trip.

The most popular method of payment (multiple answers were allowed) was credit card payment (84 mentions) followed by transfer (paperbound and online) with 65 mentions and debit entry with 41 mentions. More sophisticated methods like payment via E-Mail (PayPal) are used with a lesser frequency (only 18 mentions)).

Being asked to choose a desired payment method for the settlement of transactions in the tourism industry, responses were almost congruent with those given in the previous question. The first three most desired payment methods are again, credit card (78 mentions), transfer (65 mentions) and debit entry (27 mentions). Respondents also had the possibility to choose other payment options. This response was only made twice.

This indicates that customers (or at least the majority of all respondents) seem to be pleased with the payment options offered today. The results of question 15 ('I think that most web sites offer easy and secure methods of payment') support this assumption. 62, 4% of all respondents agreed to this statement.

Profile of respondents	
Characteristics	**Statistics**
Gender	
Male	59 (54,1%)
Female	50 (45,9%)
Age	
Mean	33,05
Standard Deviation	13,008
Education	
Hauptschulabschluss	2 (1,8%)
Realschulabschluss	8 (7,3%)
Abitur	45 (41,3%)
Bachelor	14 (12,8%)
Diplom	35 (32,1%)
Master	5 (4,6%)
Income	
less than 1.500 €	53 (48,6%)
1.500 - 2.500 €	17 (15,6%)
2.500 - 3.500 €	15 (13,8%)
3.500 - 4.500 €	11 (10,1%)
4.500 - 5.500 €	4 (3,7%)
more than 5.500 €	9 (8,3%)
Familiarity with the Internet	
less familiar	5 (4,6%)
familiar	46 (42,2%)
very familiar	58 (53,2%)
Experience with booking via the Internet	
No	10 (9,2%)
Yes	99 (90,8%)
Average spending per person and trip	
100 - 400 €	7 (6,4%)
400 - 600 €	28 (25,7%)
600 - 1.000 €	35 (32,1%)
1.000 - 2.000 €	30 (27,5%)
more than 2.000 €	9 (8,3%)

Table 1: Demographic profile of respondents

5.2 Analysis of Measurement Model

The analysis of the data gathered was twofold. First the author examined the measurement model in terms of convergent and discriminant validity. The next step dealt with the examination of the structural model aimed at identifying the strength and direction of the three constructs Perceived Trust (PT), Perceived Ease of Use (PEOU) and Perceived Usefulness (PU).

5.2.1 Convergent and discriminant validity

The statistical analysis was performed using SPSS PASW 17.0 and AMOS 5.0. First of all, discriminant and convergent validity was tested applying AVE (average variance extracted). As suggested by Fornell and Larcker (Shih, 2004), 'the average variances extracted should exceed 0.5, which indicates a good convergent and discriminant validity'. Except for three items (Search for relevant information is easy, Bookings without time restrictions and Transparency) all other items achieved a satisfactory value between ,505 and ,717.

5.2.2 Model Fit Analysis

After the application of AVE to the model, an analysis of model fitness was performed using AMOS 5.0. The overall goodness of fit was assessed using the chi-square test. 'The chi-square test assesses the adequacy of a hypothesized model in terms of its ability to reflect variance and covariance of the data. Due to its tendency to be sensitive to sample size the following indices were also applied' (Lee, 2009).

The author focussed on the fit indices GFI (Goodness-of-Fit) and AGFI (Adjusted-Goodness-of-Fit) developed by Jöreskog and Sörbom. All GFI (goodness-of-fit) values for the three constructs (PU, PEOU, and PT) were close to or greater than the 'recommended limits of .80' (Ahn et al., 2007). 'Since these fit-indices can vary, especially when being applied to smaller samples', Jöreskog, Sörbom and Bentler (Hadjar, 2004) proposed the application of two other alternative fit indices, namely RMR (Root Mean Squared Residual) and RMSEA (Root Mean Square Error of Approximation). As with the two former indices GFI and AGFI, RMR and RMSEA were also close to or even below the recommended value, which was <.10. Furthermore, the proposed model excelled in χ^2/d.f. since all values were (significantly) below the 'recommended cut-off value <5' (Ahn et al., 2007).

All three constructs have been analysed using the Kaiser-Meyer-Olkin (KMO) Measure of Adequacy. 'High KMO-values generally indicate that a factor analysis may be useful' (Brosius, 2008). All KMO-values were above the critical recommended value of .5. Furthermore, Bartlett's Test of Sphericity has been applied to all three constructs. The intention of this test is again, 'to determine whether factor analysis may be useful with the given data input. Generally, small values <0,05 indicate that a factor analysis may be useful' (Brosius, 2008). All three constructs had a value of ,000, thus were adequate for factor analysis. In addition to this, the author also produced anti-image matrixes for all three constructs. In all three cases, a large amount of factors were close to zero which indicated that the data is suited for factor analysis. Additionally, all three constructs had high MSA-indices between .0597 and .918. The MSA-index serves as a supporting instrument for the results of the KMO measure. Since both values achieved acceptable values, the factor model is accepted.

Model Fit	χ^2	df	χ^2 needed if p > 0,995	χ^2/df	GFI	AGFI	RMR	RMSEA	AVE	KMO	Bartlett	MSA
Perceived Usefulness	86,915	21	41,40	4,139	,799	,732	,125	,170		,621	,000	
H13 (PU)									,512			,789
H14 (PU)									,641			,772
H15 (PU)									,505			,861
H16 (PU)									,463			,817
H9b (PU)									,618			,713
H10b (PU)									,228			,889
H11b (PU)									,530			,834
Perceived Ease of Use	76,880	28	50,99	2,746	,857	,816	,078	,127		,504	,000	
H4 (PEOU)									,637			,743
H5 (PEOU)									,717			,760
H6a (PEOU)									,575			,918
H7 (PEOU)									,620			,916
H8 (PEOU)									,694			,870
H9 (PEOU)									,646			,769
H10a (PEOU)									,645			,769
H11a (PEOU)									,455			,903
H12a (PEOU)									,622			,895
Perceived Trust	133,296	28	50,99	4,761	,760	,691	,115	,187		,598	,000	
H6b (PT)									,522			,831
H12b (PT)									,608			,877
H17 (PT)									,715			,599
H18 (PT)									,680			,839
H19 (PT)									,702			,597
H20 (PT)									,651			,739
H21 (PT)									,511			,775
H22 (PT)									,619			,797

Table 2: Model Fit Analysis

5.3 Hypothesis Testing

Hypotheses	(very) important	Less important
H4: Speed	78,9%	6,4%
H5: Simplicity	93,2%	0%
H6: Easy and Secure Payment Methods	62,4%	13,8%
H7: Familiarity with the Internet	95,4%	4,6%
H8: Experience with online bookings	90,8%	9,2%
H9: Access to updated Availabilities	90,9%	0,9%
H10: No time restrictions (e.g. opening times)	82,7%	8,2%
H11: Search for relevant information is easy	59,6%	15,6%
H12: Web design	71,6%	6,4%
H13: Access to variety of companies / offers	86,3%	0%
H14: Booking via the Internet saves time	66,3%	17,3%
H15: Timeliness of information affects purchasing decision	70%	9,1%
H16: Transparency of offers	92,7%	0%
H17: Security and encryption of connection	91,8%	1,8%
H18: Reputation of the company	79,8%	2,7%
H19: Security of private data	91,7%	1,8%
H20: I trust my current network security	61,8%	
H21: Security of privacy affects purchasing decision	72,7%	9,1%
H22: Online sellers are trustworthy	44,1%	16,2%

Table 3: Frequencies of cumulative positive and negative responses per item (in %)

				Dependent Variable				
				Using e-Commerce for holiday bookings is				
	easy			Secure			useful	
PEOU	βs[a]	Adjusted R²	PT	βs[a]	Adjusted R²	PU	βs[a]	Adjusted R²
IV		,209	IV		,202	IV		,131
H7	-,143		H12b	,173		H13	-,107	
H8	-,162		H6b	-,126		H9b	,066	
H5	-,018		H19	,151		H10b	-,048	
H4	,217		H17	,197		H16	,357	
H9a	,175		H18	,089		H11b	,094	
H10a	-,065		H22	,063		H14	-,013	
H12a	,162		H20	,091		H15	,069	
H11a	,319		H21	,065				
H6a	,047							

Table 4: Regression results for all three model constructs

[a] Standardized β coefficient

5.4 Regression Analysis

Like other researchers, the author also applied 'multiple regression analysis in order to test possible antecedent-consequence relationships in the applied model' (comp. Shih, 2004).

5.4.1 Perceived Ease of Use

Six out of the total nine items were found to have a strong influence on Perceived Ease of Use (PEOU). Especially hypotheses 11a (Search for relevant information is easy) was found to have a strong positive influence on PEOU. All in all, hypotheses H7, H8, H4, H9a, H12a and H11a were supported. Hypotheses H5, H10a and H6a were not supported. The regression model explained 20, 9 % of the variances in PEOU of e-Commerce in the tourism industry.

5.4.2 Perceived Trust

Four out of eight items were found to have a strong influence on Perceived Trust (PT). After the analysis, hypotheses H6b, H12b, H19 and H17 were strongly supported. Hypotheses H18, H22, H20, and H21 were weakly supported. The regression model explained 20,2 % of the variances in PT of e-Commerce in the tourism industry.

5.4.3 Perceived Usefulness

Only two out of seven items were found to have a strong influence on PU. Particularly item H16 had a strong positive influence on Perceived Usefulness (PU). Hypotheses H13 and H16 were supported, whereas hypotheses H9b, H10b, H11b, H14 and H15 were weakly supported. The regression model explained only 13, 1 % of the variances in PU of e-Commerce in the tourism industry.

			Dependent Variable						
			Ability to book holidays via the Internet (Users Intention to use)						
PEOU	$βs^a$	Adjusted R²	PT	$βs^a$	Adjusted R²	PU	$βs^a$	Adjusted R²
IV		,034	IV		,346	IV		,119
H7	-,068		H12b	,045		H13	,156	
H8	,069		H6b	,000		H9b	,182	
H5	,088		H19	-,013		H10b	-,068	
H4	-,062		H17	,091		H16	,244	
H9a	,201		H18	,526		H11b	,049	
H10a	-,025		H22	,046		H14	,199	
H12a	,189		H20	-,051		H15	-,154	
H11a	,108		H21	,105				
H6a	-,037							

Table 5: Regression Analysis Constructs - Model

The result of the regression analysis, using the three constructs and its items as independent variables and the 'Ability to conduct bookings via the Internet' (Intention to Use; INT) as being the dependent variable, especially the construct of Perceived trust seems to have a strong influence on users' intention to use e-Commerce in the tourism industry. The regression model explained 34, 6% of the variances on users' intention to use e-Commerce. Particularly the item H18 (Reputation of a company) seems to have a very strong positive influence on users' intention to use e-

Commerce (β= .526). Regarding the two remaining constructs, a much weaker influence on Intention to Use is suggested. Perceived Usefulness (PU) explained 11,9% and Perceived Ease of Use (PEOU) only 3, 4% of the variances on Intention to Use. Besides the reputation of a company (H18), items like transparency (H16 -> PU; β= .244), bookings via the Internet saves me time (H14 -> PU; β= .199), quick access to updated availabilities (H9b -> PU; β= .182), and access to a variety of information (H 13 -> PU; β= .156) had a strong influence on Intention to Use. Within the construct of Perceived Ease of Use (PEOU), quick access to updated availabilities (H9a -> PEOU; β= .201), Website usability (H12 a -> PEOU; β= .189) and search for relevant information is easy (H11a -> PEOU; β= .108) were found to have the strongest influence on Intention to Use.

In the construct of Perceived Trust (PT), security of privacy (H21 -> PT; β= .105) were the only item next to H18 that had a significant influence on Intention to Use.

5.5 Results Perceived Usefulness (PU)

The following questions from the survey are assigned to the variable of 'Perceived Usefulness' (PU). As mentioned before, PU is described as 'the degree to which one believes that using a particular system or technology will enhance his or her performance' (Davies in Shih, 2004). In the context of the application of e-Commerce to tourism it is better to describe PU as the facilitating side effects of the application of a particular system.

Aspects like time savings, the provision of updated availability reports (interface), access to a wide range of products, transparency of offers and products and the ability to conduct bookings without being restricted to opening times (compared to the booking process in an ordinary travel agency) are suggested to be factors facilitating the booking process for the customer. Thus, positive ratings in these questions lead to an increase in the perceived usefulness of a system.

Summarizing the results of the questionnaire in terms of PU, it can be pointed out that customers strongly desire transparency and access to updated product availabilities. Both questions achieved an overall rating in terms of importance of over 90% and both managed to be rated as being very important by more than 50% of all respondents. With an average cumulative importance of 76, 5% of all six items surveyed it can be assumed that PU will definitely have a positive effect on users' intention to use e-Commerce in the tourism industry. However, this can only be realized under the precondition that these requests are being met on the part of participating companies in the area of the online tourism industry.

Furthermore, it is not surprising under these results, that the question 'How important is personal consultation (e.g. travel agency) for you?' is being assigned a comparably low percentage in terms of importance (only 42, 3%). This question can be regarded as the testing question for this variable. Customers, who value the facilitating factors of e-Commerce, will no longer seek for personal consultation any more. There has not been the possibility, technology-wise, to offer personal consultation in combination with e-Commerce at the same time yet. Nevertheless, many customers are still aiming to benefit from both sides of the monitor. Those customers are being informed by their travel agent in a personal consultation but might book this trip from home, looking for a bargain. On the other side, many customers do also use the internet to inform themselves about their desired holiday and then book via their local travel agency. According to the V-I-R (Verband Internet Reisevertrieb,2007) 39% of the German population aged 14 years or older are using the Internet in order to inform themselves about holidays. However, only 19 % are actually conducting bookings via the Internet.

Relating this statistic to the outcomes of the questionnaire for the variable PU, one can assume that the aspect of personal consultation plays a big role for those customers still hesitating from using the Internet for holiday or travel bookings.

5.6 Results Perceived Ease-Of-Use (PEOU)

Davies (Shih, 2004) described PEOU as 'the degree to which one believes that using a particular system would be free from effort'. Flavián et al. (2006) were using the term usability for that what has previously been defined as Perceived Ease of Use by Davies. Amongst others, the speed with which users can find what they are looking for, the simplicity of website use and the perceived ease of site navigation have been assigned to the aspect of usability. Respondents were asked to evaluate the importance of the above mentioned attributes in the survey.

A variety of questions from the questionnaire relate to this variable, containing aspects of usability and computer literacy. Flavián et al. (2006) suggested that 'greater usability has a positive influence on user satisfaction and this also generates greater website loyalty'.

Companies who want to participate in online transactions need to consider every technological and design aspect that can assist the customer in the process of finding the right web site, performing information gathering and conducting the booking. Those aspects include speed, simplicity, updated information concerning the availability of holiday components and information search. Furthermore, demographic and user-specific aspects like the familiarity with the Internet and experiences with bookings made via the Internet need to be considered.

The latter two are probably the most important ones, since they determine the customers' level of awareness, his or her level or ability to comprehend and use the system (e.g. Internet, search engines, payment method, etc.) accordingly and eliminates potential barriers of technophobia concerning the use of this medium. Once a customer has gone through the process of booking a trip via the Internet he will assumingly be easier convinced to repeat the purchase via the web site of an online seller. The companies do not have to explain the process to the customer any more.

The process of site navigation, information gathering and booking can also be regarded as every individual users' heuristic experimental testing. The more often a user iterates the whole booking process, the more likely is the development of a certain routine. This routine will also increase the users' self-confidence. Flavián et al. (2006) argue that 'greater self-confidence improves consumer trust in a website'.

Referring to the data gathered in the course of the survey, it becomes obvious that the aspect of Perceived Usefulness (PU) needs to receive more attention in the future. Especially attributes like simplicity and availability of updated vacancies have received a very high rating in terms of importance. More than 90% of all responses evaluated those two attributes as being very important (53,2%; 50, 9%) or important (44%; 40%).

5.7 Results Perceived Trust (PT)

As mentioned before, trust and the perception of safety and security are regarded as being the essential ingredients for a 'tasty and successful e-Commerce dish'. According to Flavián et al. (2006), 'trust has a notable influence on the attainment of long-lasting and profitable relationships'. Respondents were asked to assign ratings to the perceived security and trust within their current online shopping activities.

The responses to this construct were more diversified than those given to the two previous constructs PU and PEOU. Apparently, respondents were cautious in their answers to the questions assigned to this construct. There were a few items that attained a comparable low rating in terms of importance or agreement. Amongst them, the trustworthiness of online sellers has being assigned the lowest agreement. Only 44, 1 % of all respondents agreed to the statement, that online sellers are trustworthy. Whereas in turn, 16, 2% disagreed with this statement. Furthermore, respondents seem to be concerned with the security of their current network. 12,7 % of all persons surveyed stated, that they disagree with the statement, that their current network is secure.

Summarizing the outcomes for this construct, it can be argued that there are different responsibilities and institutions involved in the process of improving the trustworthiness of e-Commerce in tourism as a whole. On the one hand, the security of the IT-infrastructure needs to be improved, since customers doubt the actual level of security. This can also be manifested by the outcomes concerning the needs of the customers to secure their private data. Over 90% of all respondents stated that the security of their private data is being important to them. So there will be an increasing need for more security. First attempts to improve it might possibly be done via the introduction of the new electronical passport in Germany in 2010. Biometrical data will be saved on the new passport facilitating trade via the Internet. However, as with all new technologies there is an increasing risk of fraud and misuse.

On the other hand, companies need to work on their credibility and trustworthiness. This can be achieved through security or trust seals displayed on the companies' Website. This would indicate that the company complies to the rules and regulations established of the issuing organisation. However, one can of course argue that the

[...] 'seals may be no more than marketing ploys to lull consumers into a false sense of security' (Bhasin, 2006). A prominent example for trust seals is 'WebTrust, which was jointly introduced by the American Institute of Certified Public Accountants (AICPA) and the Canadian Institute of Chartered Accountants (CICA)' (Lala et al., 2002). However, WebTrust did not manage to reach a critical mass since its introduction. According to Lala et al. (2002), one reason for the 'poor market penetration is that consumers are unable to differentiate between the information quality of different Internet seals'. In other words, due to the numerous providers of online seals, it is almost impossible to differentiate between them and to detect potential fraudster or dubious providers.

This problem could be solved by a strong cooperation consisting of online sellers like eBay or Amazon, credit card companies like VISA and MasterCard and regulatory and governmental institutions. Through the participation of the 'big players' in both, the online market and credit card suppliers, a critical mass can be achieved quickly which might lead to the establishment of an industry standard. This would assure that those companies being assigned with the trust seal can be trusted. In case those companies fail to comply with the rules and regulations they will have to face considerable penalties.

5.8 Results open-ended questions

Question 12 of the questionnaire provided respondents with the opportunity to include more qualitative and subjective information. The most meaningful comments dealt with topics of transparency, simplicity , Web design, security of private data, IT infrastructure, advertising and personal contact.

5.8.1 Transparency

The majority of open-ended responses focussed on the topic of transparency. It was obvious that respondents increasingly ask for more price transparency in order to increase the comparability of companies and offers. Furthermore, respondents would like to have a clear pricing with no hidden costs (respondent referred to Ryan Air).

5.8.2 Simplicity

To a large extend, respondents indicated that they would appreciate a better Web site usability including particularly aspects like site navigation and search functions.

5.8.3 IT infrastructure
Some respondents were complaining about incidents where the Internet connection broke down during the actual booking process which has been very annoying.

5.8.4 Personal Contact (Consultation)
Some respondents were missing personal consultation or at least a contact person where they could address their questions to, especially when it comes to bookings that afford special destination know-how. Respondents also asked for toll-free service numbers.

5.8.5 Linkages between offer and feedback of previous, experienced customers
The people surveyed were also very interested in the possibility of linking customer feedback directly to offers.

5.8.6 Advertising
A few customers were annoyed by too much advertisement on the Web sites. To a large extent, theses respondents were elderly people (e.g. 74 years old).

6. Discussion
The study explored the strength of the adjusted TAM and its three constructs. The main part of hypotheses could be supported, although some of them had to be rejected after the statistical analysis. It also aids in identifying the most influential items in each construct. Especially H11a (Search for relevant information is easy -> PEOU), H17 (Transfer of transaction details via an encrypted and secure connection -> PT) and H 16 (Transparency of companies and offers -> PU) seem to have a strong positive influence on the constructs. In contrast to similar studies, Perceived Trust (PT) emerged as the most influential predictor of e-Commerce acceptance in the tourism industry when comparing the adjusted R^2 values of the three constructs. PT explained 34, 6% of the variance on users' intention to use e-Commerce. Prior studies always identified Perceived Usefulness to be the most influential predictor of e-Commerce acceptance (e.g. Ha & Stoel, 2009). This inconsistency calls for further research in this area. However, in terms of the number of influencing items, the construct Perceived Usefulness (PU) delivered the highest amount. Five out of seven variables indicated a significant positive and negative influence on users' intention to use e-Commerce in the tourism industry. This would complement the outcomes of previous studies.

Regarding the frequency of positively and negatively rated responses concerning importance and agreement, the study identified that respondents were especially concerned with the current security of their network and the trustworthiness of online sellers. The strong path coefficient of H17 (Transfer of transaction details via an encrypted and secure connection) could also be verified by the importance assigned to this item on the side of the respondents.

The outcome that Perceived Trust seemed to be the most influential construct in the adapted TAM leads to the conclusion that advances in technology also involve more complex processes and a better and sophisticated understanding and knowledge of the customers. The key element in further enhancing e-Commerce in the tourism industry lies mainly in the area of simplicity and security. In terms of security, customers are even willing to sacrifice certain aspects. According to a recent study of the Verband Internet Reisevertrieb (2009), 14% (out of 1104 persons surveyed) would accept higher costs and 31% would accept longer waiting within the transaction process given an improvement in security. These findings indicate the perceived importance of security to customers. It should be of future common interest to create awareness and understanding for the different payment methods offered by online sellers.

This would also involve IT infrastructure education. Many customers simply do not know enough concerning security enhancing technologies and trust seals, or soft- and hardware components that can improve the security of online transactions. Similar to what is already offered in the cruise industry, so-called e-Security campuses should be introduced to the customer. As with the example of the cruise campus (www.cruisecampus.de) a comparable Web site can improve the knowledge of voluntary participants. This could be one way to enhance the overall awareness of customers about security and payment issues in the world of e-Business.

Furthermore, the whole industry (online sellers) should aim to introduce an industry standard consisting of rules and regulations. On the basis of these guiding principles, companies complying with them should be rewarded with the assignment of a Europe-wide and valid trust seal. In turn, companies failing to comply with the rules need to face severe penalties. This would enhance the participation of online sellers in the process of security improvements.

7. Limitations of this work

Limitations of this work mainly concern the surveyed sample. Although the range in terms of age distribution was large (55 years) the majority of all respondents was comparable young (aged between 19 and 32). Furthermore, the surveyed sample had on average a very high level of computer- / Internet-literacy and most of the respondents did already perform bookings via the Internet. It would be worthwhile to apply the model to a population that does not have made experiences with the Internet so far. The author believes, that this outcome would indicate differences compared with the results of the current survey. Moreover, the sample size (n=109) might not be representative, although comparable research in this area was also conducted with smaller samples between 100 – 400 respondents. Other demographic limitations include the income level of respondents. Since most of the people participating in the survey where students, the survey yielded a low average income level with over 48% earning less than 1.500 € per month.

In addition to this, the model applied might not fully cover the whole range of aspects determining customers' acceptance and intention to use e-Commerce in the tourism industry. Further aspects that can be analysed and added to the concept used will be highlighted in the next section.

8. Further Research

The author points out that the outcomes of this work should not serve as a basis for generalization. They should rather insert new knowledge and outcomes into the ongoing research undertaken in the area of technology acceptance, and especially within the application of e-Commerce in the tourism industry. The results aim to supplement prior and future research.

Potential areas for further research are on the one hand the limitations of this work. For example, an application of this model to a larger and perhaps more differentiated sample would deliver valuable results. Other authors should especially consider its application to populations consisting of people with no or limited computer or Internet knowledge/experience. In addition to this, applying the model to populations with no permanent Internet access (e. g. Senior citizens, handicapped persons, etc.) might provide researchers with new outcomes. Furthermore, since the questionnaire could only be answered by German-speaking respondents, there is plenty of room to apply it to other countries or populations with different technological, cultural and educational backgrounds.

Other interesting questions are customer website loyalty or respectively, switching costs for websites. Do users stick with one website after a successful completed transaction? What can be done in order to increase switching costs for e-Tourism customers? Which roles play customer profiles and customisation of offers?

9. Acknowledgements

The author would like to thank his family members for their support and valuable comments that contributed to the establishment of the questionnaire. Furthermore many thanks to Professor Alexis Papathanassis who was very supportive and helped steering this work into the right direction.

Bibliography

Books

- Brosius, F. (2008) SPSS 16 – Das mitp-Standardwerk. REDLINE GMBH: Heidelberg
- Dannenberg, M. & Ulrich, A. (2004) E-Payment und E-Billing Elektronische Bezahlsysteme für Mobilfunk und Internet. Betriebswirtschaftlicher Verlag Dr. Th. Gabler /GWV Fachverlage GmbH: Wiesbaden
- Hadjar, A. (2004) Ellenbogenmentalität und Fremdenfeindlichkeit bei Jugendlichen. VS Verlag für Sozialwissenschaften / GWV Fachverlage GmbH: Wiesbaden
- Lammer, T. (2006) HANDBUCH E-Money, E-Payment & M-Payment. Physica-Verlag Heidelberg: Heidelberg
- Lawrence, D. & Tavakol, S. (2007) Balanced Website Design – Optimising Aesthetics, Usability and Purpose. Springer Verlag: London.
- Schultz, C. D. (2007) Consumer Trust in E-Commerce. Verlag Dr. Kovač: Hamburg
- Stahl, E., Krabichler, T., Breitschaft, M. & Wittmann, G. (2008) E-Commerce-Leitfaden – Erfolgreich im Elektronischen Handel. Universitätsverlag Regensburg: Regensburg

Internet

- Böhle, K., Krueger, M., Hermann, C., Carat, G. & Maghiros, I. (2000) Electronic Payment Systems – Strategic and Technical Issues – Background Paper No.1 Electronic Payment Systems Observatory (ePSO). Retrieved May 21, 2009 from the World Wide Web: http://citeseerx.ist.psu.edu/viewdoc/summary?doi=10.1.1.24.2198
- DRV Deutscher Reiseverband (2008). DRV_Zahlen_Fakten_2008.pdf. Retrieved May 28, 2009 from the World Wide Web: http://www.drv.de/fileadmin/user_upload/fachbereiche/DRV_Zahlen_Fakten_2008.pdf
- PayPal (2009). Welcome to PayPal. Retrieved May 28, 2009 from the World Wide Web: https://www.paypal.com/uk/cgi-bin/webscr?cmd=_home-general&nav=0
- VIR Verband Internet Reisevertrieb (2007). v-i-r Daten und Fakten 2 2007. Retrieved March24, 2009 from the World Wide Web: http://www.v-i-r.de/cms/upload/downloads/vir/v-i-r-daten-und-fakten-2-2007.pdf

- VIR Verband Internet Reisevertrieb (2009). *v-i-r Daten und Fakten 2009.* Retrieved July 11, 2009 from the World Wide Web: http://www.v-i-r.de/cms/upload/bilder/Daten/df09s.pdf
- Wikipedia (2009). *Lastschrift.* Retrieved May 28, 2009 from the World Wide Web: http://de.wikipedia.org/wiki/Lastschrift
- Wordnet Princeton University (2006). *Trust.* Retrieved July 12, 2009 from the World Wide Web: http://wordnetweb.princeton.edu/perl/webwn?s=trust

Journals

- Ahn, T., Ryu, S. & Han, I. (2007). The impact of Web quality and playfulness on user acceptance of online retailing. *Information & Management, 44 (3),* 263 – 275. DOI: 10.1016/j.im.2006.12.008
- Ashrafi, M. Z. & Ng, S. K. (2009). Privacy-preserving e-payments using one-time payment details. *Computer Standards & Interfaces, 31 (2),* 321 – 328. DOI: 10.1016/j.csi.2008.04.001
- Bhasin, M. L. (2006). Guarding Privacy on the Internet. *Global Business Review 7,* 137 – 156. DOI: 10.1177/097215090500700109#
- Chadwick, S. A. (2001). Communicating Trust in E-Commerce Interactions. *Management Communication Quarterly, 14,* 653-658. DOI: 10.1177/0893318901144009
- Cheyne, J., Downes, M. & Legg, S. (2006). Travel agent vs. Internet: What influences travel consumer choices? *Journal of Vacation Marketing 12 (1),* 41 – 57. DOI: 10.1177/1356766706059307
- Corry, M. D., Frick, T. W. & Hansen, L. (1997). User-centered Design and Usability Testing of a Web Site: An Illustrative Case Study. *ETR&D 45 (4),* 65-76
- Flavián, C., Guinalíu, M. & Gurrea, R. (2006). The role played by perceived usability, satisfaction and consumer trust on website loyalty. *Information & Management 43 (1),* 1-14. DOI: 10.1016/j.im.2005.01.002
- Gadhzeva, M. (2008). Privacy in the Age of Transparency: The new Vulnerability of the Individual. *Social Science Computer Review 26 (60),* 60-74. DOI: 10.1177/0894439307307686
- Ha, S. & Stoel, L. (2009). Consumer e-shopping acceptance: Antecedents in a technology acceptance model. *Journal of Business Research 62 (5),* 565-571. DOI: 10.1016/j.jbusres.2008.06.016
- Hinde, S. (1998). Privacy and Security – The Drivers for Growth of E-Commerce. *Computers & Security 17,* 475-478. DOI: 10.1016/S0167-4048(98)80069-2

- Yu, H.-C., Hsi, K.-H. & Kuo, P.-J. (2002). Electronic payment systems: an analysis and comparison of types. *Technology in Society 24 (3)*, 331-347. DOI: 10.1016/S0160-791X(02)00012-X

- Kim, H.-B., Kim, T. & Shin, S. W. (2009). Modelling roles of subjective norms and eTrust in customers' acceptance of airline B2C e-Commerce websites. *Tourism Management 30 (2)*, 266-277. DOI: 10.1016/j.tourman.2008.07.001

- Koufaris, M. & Hampton-Sosa, W. (2004). The development of initial trust in an online company by new customers. *Information & Management 41 (3)*, 377-397. DOI: 10.1016/j.im.2003.08.004

- Lai, V. S. & Li, H. (2005). Technology acceptance model for internet banking: an invariance analysis. *Information & Management 42 (2)*, 373 – 386. DOI: 10.1016/j.im.2004.01.007

- Lala, V., Arnold, V., Sutton, S. G. & Guan, L. (2002). The impact of relative information quality of e-commerce assurance seals on Internet purchasing behavior. *International Journal of Accounting Information Systems 3 (4)*, 237 – 253. DOI: 10.1016/S1467-0895(02)00069-6

- Landrock, P. (2002). Security – The Building Block for e-Commerce Growth. *Computer Fraud & Security 9*, 7-8. DOI: 10.1016/S1361-3723(02)00910-7

- Lang, T.C. (2000). The effect of the Internet on Travel Consumer Purchasing Behavior and Implications for Travel Agencies. *Journal of Vacation Marketing 6*, 368 – 385. DOI: 10.1177/135676670000600407

- Lee, M.-C. (2009). Factors influencing the adoption of internet banking: An integration of TAM and TPB with perceived risk and perceived benefit. *Electronic Commerce Research and Applications 8*, 130-141. DOI: 10.1016/j.elerap.2008.11.006

- Morgan, N. J., Pritchard, A. & Abbott, S. (2001). Consumers, travel and technology: A bright future for the Web or television shopping? *Journal of Vacation Marketing 7*, 110-124. DOI: 10.1177/135676670100700202

- Palvia, P. (2009). The role of trust in e-Commerce relational exchange: A unified model. *Information & Management 46 (4)*, 213-220. DOI: 10.1016/j.im.2009.02.003

- Park, N., Roma, R., Lee, S. & Chung, J. E. (2009). User acceptance of a digital library system in developing countries: An Application of the Technology Acceptance Model. *International Journal of Information Management 29 (3)*, 196-209. DOI: 10.1016/j.ijinfomgt.2008.07.001

- Porter, M. (2001). Strategy and the Internet. *Harvard Business Review 79 (3)*, 62-78.

- Shankar, V., Urban, G. L. & Sultan, F. (2002) Online trust: a stakeholder perspective, concepts, implications, and future directions. *The Journal of Strategic Information Systems 11 (3-4)*, 325 – 344. DOI: 10.1016/S0963-8687(02)00022-7

- Shih, H.-P. (2004). An empirical study on predicting user acceptance of e-shopping on the Web. *Information & Management 41 (3)*, 351-368. DOI: 10.1016/S0378-7206(03)00079-X

- Stroborn, K., Heitmann, A., Leibold, K. & Frank, G. (2004). Internet Payments in Germany: a classificatory framework and empirical evidence. *Journal of Business Research 57 (12)*, 1431-1437. DOI: 10.1016/S0148-2963(02)00433-2

- Talwatte, G. (2000). E-Commerce is key to global competitiveness – but is there anyone you can trust in the online world? *Business Information Review 17*, 78-81. DOI: 10.1177/0266382004237557

- Vijayasarathy, L. R. (2004). Predicting consumer intentions to use on-line shopping: the case for an augmented technology acceptance model. *Information & Management 41 (6)*, 747 – 762. DOI: 10.1016/j.im.2003.08.011

- Zviran, M., Glezer, C. & Avni, I. (2006). User satisfaction from commercial web sites: The effect of design and use. *Information & Management 43 (2)*, 157 – 178. DOI: 10.1016/j.im.2005.04.002

Printed in Great Britain
by Amazon.co.uk, Ltd.,
Marston Gate.